Canticle of the Cross

by Joseph

Chamber Orchestration by Brant Adams

Contents

Program notes are on page 76.

Performance Time: approximately 30 minutes

(1) This symbol indicates a track number on the StudioTrax CD (Accompaniment Only).

Harold Flammer
M U S I C

A DIVISION OF SHAWNEE PRESS, INC.

EXCLUSIVELY DISTRIBUTED BY HAL LEONARD CORPORATION

Visit Shawnee Press Online at
www.shawneepress.com

Foreword

The cross waited in utter silence, her unmoving limbs empty and barren. Her form was bent and broken, fashioned by uncaring hands into a scaffold of shame. Soon, lost and violent men would raise her rugged timbers into the unforgiving skies of Jerusalem. In their anger and fury they would plunge heavy nails into her bark and fasten a condemned man onto her frame. She waits in the shadows while the chilling winds of Mt. Calvary begin to howl in agony for the one who would die in her arms.

JOSEPH M. MARTIN

Meditation

The cross of Christ
is a pillar of truth to guide me.

The cross of Christ
is a shield to overshadow me.

The cross of Christ
is a tower of strength to protect me.

The cross of Christ
goes before and behind me.

The cross of Christ
is above and beneath me.

The cross of Christ
is on my left and on my right.

The cross of Christ
is within and about me.

How wonderful the cross of Christ!

It brings life, not death;
light, not darkness.

It is the wood on which the Lord,
like a great Warrior, was wounded
and died for the sin of the world.

A tree had destroyed us;
a tree now brings us life.

PROLOGUE

Based on tune: **DYMA GARIA**
by ROBERT LOWRY (1826-1899
Arranged by
JOSEPH M. MARTIN (BMI

Not hurried, with tender expression (♩ = ca. 68)

ACCOMP.

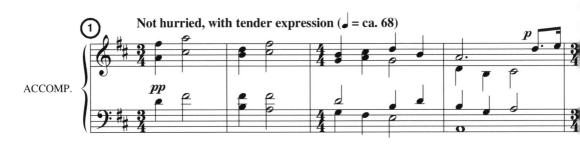

commissioned by Ash Creek Baptist Church, Azle, Texas,
in honor of Connie Deweese's 25 years of dedicated service as pianist

THE SONG OF THE CROSS

Words and music by
JOSEPH M. MARTIN (BMI

SOPRANO
ALTO

From a cross far a - way comes the

song of grace, a voice filled with hope for the wea - ry. Car - ried

high on the wind like a gen-tle hymn,_____ 'tis a

song from the heart of God. Seek-ers come to Me, in My

TENOR

BASS

arms there is peace. I will sing you the song__ ev-er-

unis.

last - ing. Come to Me and rest. Be for - ev - er blest.

I will sing you the song of the cross.

Un - der - neath Love's wings, where the

shad - ows____ sing,____ where the mus - ic of all life is cre -

a tempo **30**

at - ed.____ Like a whis - pered __ prayer, grace is

a tempo **30**

mp

wait - ing there._____ 'Tis a song from the heart____ of

God. Seek-ers, come to Me. In My arms there is peace. I will sing you the song ev - er - last - ing. Come to Me and rest. Be for - ev - er blest._____ I will

NARRATION:

As Jesus approached Jerusalem, He saw the great city and began to weep. This ancient city had known many tears in her long, troubled history. Her stone pathways were consecrated with the blood of martyrs, and her walls echoed the cries of a million prayers for deliverance. Now, as the Promised One drew near, the towering gates of the city flew open to receive her King. Crowds began to gather chanting, "Blessed is He who comes in the name of the Lord."

Running ahead, the people laid their coats upon the road as a carpet of praise to the Deliverer. They took palm branches and waved them in adoration of their conquering King. This was the day they had long-awaited, and their celebration could be heard in the temple. "Hosanna," they cried, "Hosanna to the Son of David!"

commissioned by the Sanctuary Choir of Belmont Baptist Church, Charlottesville, Virginia,
to the glory of God and in honor of Gloria Johnson for 40 faithful years of service as organist

A CELTIC HOSANNA

Words by
JOSEPH M. MARTIN

Based on tune: **ST. DENIO**
Traditional Welsh Tune
Arranged by
JOSEPH M. MARTIN (BMI)

way; and shout to the na-tions: "the King has come— to-

day."

The—

Shield and De-fend-er the An-cient of Days_____ has come to His peo-ple to rule and_____ to_____ reign. Ho - san - na, ho - san - na._____ Ho -

NARRATION:

Jesus and his followers lingered in the temple where He continued to teach them a new way. The people treasured every word, but the Chief Priests, scribes and elders tried to disrupt His preaching. "Look how the whole world seems to be following Him," they said.

Jesus knew that the hour was near for Him to leave the world and return to the Father. He understood that His sacred sojourn to Jerusalem had been a steady, unrelenting procession to the cross.

Later, as He gathered with His chosen ones for Passover, Jesus broke bread and blessed it. "Take and eat. This is My body."

He poured wine into a chalice and gave it to them and said, "This is the blood of the covenant which is poured out for many."

How could they have known that even in their final hymn of benediction, He was once again teaching them of grace? For saturating every holy word He chanted, and lavished upon each solemn note He sang, was the bittersweet song of the cross.

COME TO THE UPPER ROOM

Words by
JOSEPH M. MARTIN

Traditional English Melody
Arranged by
JOSEPH M. MARTIN (BMI)

home in the heart of the Sav - ior. Come to the up - per __ room.

There's a ban - quet of hope __ for the hun - gry. Come to the up - per __

Christ will give you peace._____ There's a

home in the heart of the Sav - ior. Come to the up - per_

room. Come and eat the bread of re - demp - tion. Come and

drink the wine that re - stores._____ Come re-

ceive heav-en's grace that is ev - er - last - ing.

Come and taste all the good - ness of the Lord.

There's a home in the heart of the Sav - ior.

Come to the up - per room. Come to the

up - per room.

NARRATION:

The Garden had always been a special place for Jesus. As He walked among the olive trees of Gethsemane, did He think of Eden and the tree that had brought death to His beloved creation? "Where are you?" He had called to His children in the cool of the day.

Now He was calling them again. By His message of grace, He was drawing His creation back to the garden. This time, the tree in the center of it all would not bring death but life everlasting. The emotion of it overwhelmed Him and He fell to the ground in anguish. Over and over He cried, "Father, let this cup pass from Me."

Then at once a deep peace flooded His spirit and He spoke, "Father, let Thy will be done." His words resounded through the lonely garden, and for a moment it seemed the evening breeze stood breathless and still.

THE GARDEN OF TEARS

Words and music by
JOSEPH M. MARTIN (BMI)
Incorporating tunes:
DIM OND IESU
LITTLE RED BIRD

Who is praying in the garden, underneath the olive trees?

Who kneels down His heart in anguish? Who cries out in agony?

(Accompanist may double voices if desired.)

* Tune: DIM OND IESU, Welsh Hymn Tune, David Emlyn Evans (1843-1913)

Je - sus, Je - sus, Pre - cious Rose, now__ crushed for__ me. Je - sus, Je - sus, Pre - cious Rose,__ now__ crushed_____ for_____

38

as from a distance

"Come a - way. Come a - way."

as from a distance

Look to the Rose of par - a - dise. O

come to the gar - den of tears.

Journey to dark Gethsemane.

Come away. Come away.

Soft on the wind, there comes a song: "Come a - way. Come a - way." "Fa - ther,

NARRATION:

He had been a Carpenter. Wood and nails had been His trade. Now, He gazed upon the wooden cross before Him, and for a moment He remembered a gentler time.

Then soldiers laid the heavy beams of the cross upon His shoulders, and at the crack of the whip, the condemned Carpenter began to walk the winding road up to the place of the skull. With each step He took, the cruel timbers beat out a rhythm of death and despair upon that stony path. The song of the cross began to moan like a dirge as the cries of a violent mob filled the air with the music of grief and sorrow. The Carpenter fell beneath the cross.

THE CARPENTER

Words by
JOSEPH M. MARTIN

Based on tune
THE STAR OF THE COUNTY DOWN
Traditional Irish Melody
Arranged by
JOSEPH M. MARTIN (BMI)

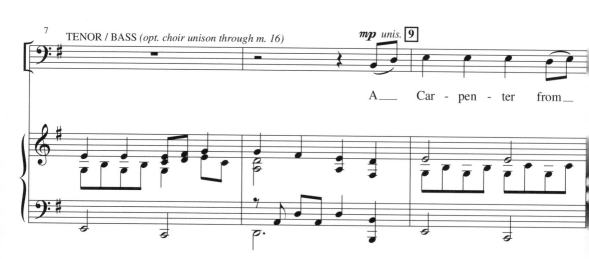

on the rug-ged wood; and spoke when all His work was done, "It is fin-ished. It is good."

The

(Tenor only)

Carpenter from Gal - i - lee soon moved to oth - er art. With lov - ing touch He healed the sick and fixed the sin - ner's heart. With thought - ful care He

50

took the nails and laid His hands to wood.

p unis.

Then

spoke in-to e-ter-ni-ty "It is fin-ished. It is

54

* The vowel sound on the initial "loo" should match the vowel sound of "good."

CANTICLE OF THE CROSS - SATB

NARRATION:

See from His hands, His head, His feet, sorrow and love flow mingled down. Did e're such love and sorrow meet, or thorns compose so rich a crown?

Isaac Watts (1674-1748)

A TREE ONCE STOOD

Words and music by
JOSEPH M. MARTIN (BMI)

cross. The pre - cious Sav - ior of the world, she

held in her em - brace. She felt the pain of

ev - 'ry nail that pierced His hands of grace.

(end solo)

day. A sil - hou - ette of sol - i - tude a -

gainst the dark - 'ning sky, with care she cra - dled

Christ the King and held Him as He cried.

See the cross___ of Christ now ris - ing, tow-'ring o - ver a world of strife. See the Sav - ior pierced and dy - ing. Christ is cru - ci - fied.___ On the cross___ He gives___ His

Cross of grief ___ and shame!___

Stately, with sadness (♩ = ca. 84)

rit.

mp

rit. *dim.*

㉗

61 **Tempo I**

p unis.

A

p unis.

61 **Tempo I**

p

tree once stood on a lone - ly hill, where love___ was cru - ci -

fied; and all may gath - er in___ its shade; and

none will be___ de - nied. No great - er tree has

ev - er grown than Cal - v'ry's cross_ di - vine. Her

out - stretched arms_ are o - pen still, re - demp - tion's grand_ de-

sign._____

28 *rit.*

rit.

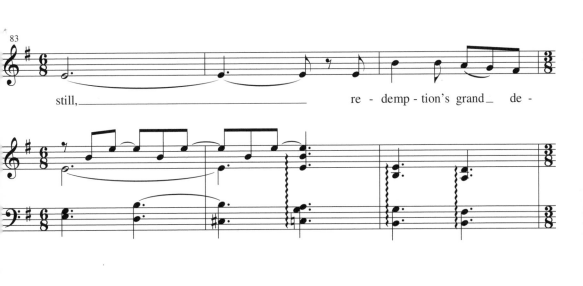

NARRATION:

The cross of Christ is a pillar of truth to guide me.

The cross of Christ is a shield to overshadow me.

The cross of Christ is a tower of strength to protect me.

The cross of Christ goes before and behind me.

The cross of Christ is above and beneath me.

The cross of Christ is on my left and on my right.

The cross of Christ is within and about me.

How wonderful the cross of Christ!

It brings life, not death; light, not darkness.

It is the wood on which the Lord, like a great Warrior, was wounded and died for the sin of the world.

A tree had destroyed us; a tree now brings us life.

The Christ of the Cross is all in all to me.

in recognition of Norm and Carol Geisbrecht's retirement
after more than 26 years of musical leadership,
Highland Baptist Church, Kitchener, Ontario

CONSOLATION OF THE CROSS

Words by
GIROLAMO SAVONAROLA (1452-1498)
Translation by
JANE WILDE (1826-1896), *alt.*

Tune: **DYMA GARIAD**
by ROBERT LOWRY (1826-1899)
Arranged by
JOSEPH M. MARTIN (BMI)

from the world a - bove; of - ten has God's heart been

bro - ken,__ think-ing on the sin-ner's fall. Now in

grace, the cross has spo - ken,__ "It is fin - ished once for

all."

(end solo)

70

thorn en - cir - cled brow? Yet Your sin - less death has brought us___ life e - ter - nal, peace and rest.___ On - ly what___ Your grace has taught us___ calms the sin - ner's deep dis

tress.

cresc. poco a poco

rit.   **mf** *unis.*

Je - sus,

mf *unis.*

rit.   **mf**

may   our   hearts   be   burn - ing___   with_ more   fer - vent   love   for

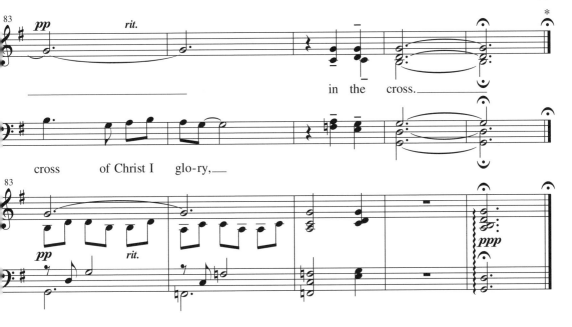

in the cross._____

cross of Christ I glo-ry,___

EPILOGUE
(optional)

Mournfully (♩ = ca. 60)   *(Repeat ad lib., fading into the distance)*

The cantata can end at m. 87 or, after a short pause, continue to the "Epilogue."

* Tune: NEW BRITAIN, *Virginia Harmony,* 1831   CANTICLE OF THE CROSS - SATB

PROGRAM NOTES

This service of song is intended to follow the path of the cross from the Triumphal Entry to the Crucifixion. The cantata, based on Celtic folksongs and Celtic-styled original songs, is designed to bring a consistent musical and artistic vernacular to the worship event.

Some directors may want to utilize extra-musical elements to enhance their presentation of *Canticle of the Cross*. Feel free to either incorporate your own creative ideas or adapt some from the suggestions listed below.

To incorporate an extra-musical element into the presentation, have your choir process behind a simple cross during the playing of the "Prologue." Place the cross upon the altar as the choir takes its place. As the narrative unfolds, the altar can be adorned progressively with symbols to represent Christ's passion. These symbols can be added at the close of each respective narration, and should be completed as the introduction of the appropriate song is beginning.

Candles may also be incorporated to show the progression of the passion. Prearrange 6 candles upon the altar leaving room for the placement of the cross. (The candles may also be free standing for a more dramatic presentation.) Light the candles during the "Prologue," during the first anthem, or before the service begins. Before each anthem, ceremoniously extinguish one candle until they all have been snuffed out, symbolizing the moment of Christ's death. The use of candles may be used with or without the use of symbols.

Below are some possible symbols to incorporate. (Feel free to substitute, based upon your own traditions.)

"The Song of the Cross" — No adornment; however if candles are used they can be brought in and lit during this first anthem.

"A Celtic Hosanna" (Palm Sunday) — a purple cloth for the base of the cross and/or palm fronds may be placed in a vase.

"Come to the Upper Room" (Last Supper) — a chalice and a loaf of bread may be brought to the altar.

"The Garden of Tears" (Gethsemane) — Red rose petals may be scattered upon the altar to represent Christ's shedding of "sweat drops as blood" in the garden.

"The Carpenter" (Ministry and Humility of Christ) — Large spikes and a wooden mallet or rustic hammer may be brought to the altar.

"A Tree Once Stood" (Crucifixion) — A black cloth may be draped over the cross.

"Consolation of the Cross" — Towards the end of this song remove the black cloth and fold it. Take the cross, then walk slowly from the sanctuary as the "Epilogue" is played. The folded black cloth follows, carried reverently as in a funeral procession. Then follow with each of the now extinguished candles, the narrator and then the choir. The congregation then exits in silence as the "Epilogue" is repeated until all congregants have left the building. If available, a lone bagpiper may stand at a distance and play the "Epilogue" as worshippers either reflect in silence, or as they depart.

Much grace...
Joseph M. Martin

FAVORITE CANTATAS FOR LENT & EASTER

THE SONG EVERLASTING

A SACRED CANTATA BASED ON EARLY AMERICAN SONGS

Joseph Martin

From the composer who brought you *Tapestry of Light*, *The Rose of Calvary* and *The Lenten Sketches*, comes a new work filled with the music of grace. The life of Christ is dramatically presented in this choral cantata that tells the gospel story using American folk songs and hymns. Filled with time-honored tunes and texts, this masterfully arranged work will connect with the congregation and choir alike.

Divided into three sections – Ministry, Humility and Victory – this cantata can be done progressively throughout Lent, Holy Week and Eastertide, or it can be performed as one large celebration of the life of Christ.

35028094	SATB	$8.95
35028163	SAB	$8.95
35028095	iPrint Full Orchestration	$350.00
35028096	Printed Full Orchestration	$350.00
35028200	iPrint Appalacian Consort	$175.00
35028097	StudioTrax CD	$80.00
35028098	Listening CD	$15.99
35028099	10-Pack Listening CDs	$65.00
35028100	Preview Pack (Book/Listening CD)	$16.99
35028101	RehearsalTrax CDs (part-predominant, reproducible)	$64.99
35028102	Digital Resource Kit	$59.99

WHISPERS OF THE PASSION

Joseph M. Martin

The creative team that brought you *The Lenten Sketches* and *Covenant of Grace* now present a work filled with intensity and passion. In this work the silent witnesses to the last days of Christ speak in 5 soliloquies that testify to the timeless message of grace. These monologues are followed by beautiful musical moments that present new anthems as well as traditional Lenten hymns. This work, designed primarily for Holy Week performance incorporates simple symbols, (Palms, Chalice, Robe, Crown of Thorns and Cross) to be presented as the work unfolds.

Whispers of the Passion is supported by a complete line of products that will add a variety of options for churches of any size. With a 30-35 minute length of performance, this flexible work can be integrated into a regular service or can even be done progressively over the weeks leading up to Good Friday.

35027674	SATB	$8.95
35027675	Printed Chamber Orchestration	$250.00
35027676	iPrint Chamber Orchestration	$250.00
35027677	StudioTrax CD	$80.00
35027678	Listening CD	$15.99
35027679	10-Pack Listening CDs	$65.00
35027680	Preview Pack (Book/Listening CD)	$16.99
35027681	RehearsalTrax CDs (part-predominant, reproducible)	$64.99
35027682	Digital Resources Kit	$59.99

THE LENTEN SKETCHES

Joseph M. Martin

From the composer of *Song of the Shadows*, *Harvest of Sorrows* and *The Weeping Tree* comes a brilliant new innovative cantata for Holy Week, *The Lenten Sketches*. The work is a series of tableaus illustrating the pivotal final days of Christ's earthly ministry, the triumphal entry, the last supper, the garden of Gethsemane and the crucifixion. With a performance time of approximately 30 minutes, the cantata is easily integrated into a worship event. There is a full line of support products available to help facilitate your presentation of this dramatic new work including a digital resource kit featuring art work, PowerPoint visuals, a Bible study, practice hints, interpretive movement options, plus a unique composer's commentary explaining some of the writer's perspective on the composition of the cantata.

35026778	SATB	$8.95
35027066	Listening CD	$15.99
35027068	Preview Pack (Book/Listening CD)	$16.99
35027067	10-Pack Listening CDs	$65.00
35027069	RehearsalTrax CDs (part-dominant, reproducible)	$64.99
35027065	StudioTrax CD	$80.00
35027064	Printed Chamber Orchestration	$250.00
35027063	iPrint Chamber Orchestration	$250.00
35027070	Digital Resources Kit	$59.99

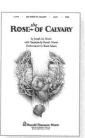

THE ROSE OF CALVARY

Joseph M. Martin/ orch. Brant Adams

The Rose of Calvary is the greatly anticipated sequel to the best-selling cantata, *The Winter Rose*. Using the same beautiful imagery, the work tells the story of Jesus's ministry, passion, death on the cross and his triumphant resurrection. This creative work has nine new anthems and contains opportunities for soloists and narrators. Written to function as either a work for Holy Week or with the optional ending as a joyful celebration of the resurrection, this musical offers maximum flexibility to the director. Brant Adams reprises his role as orchestrator, and Pamela Martin once again provides thoughtful and meaningful narration. Spectacular!

35018630	SATB	$7.95
35018633	Orchestration	$350.00
35018637	Accompaniment CD	$80.00
35018644	Listening CD	$15.98
35018638	CD 10-Pack	$65.00
35018639	CD 25-Pack	$110.00
35018631	Preview Pack (Book/CD)	$16.99

Shawnee Press

Prices, contents, and availability subject to change without notice.

HARVEST OF SORROWS
Joseph M. Martin

Through music and symbols, worshippers are invited to a season of contemplation as the mystery and power of Christ's passion are presented. Using new music and beloved hymnody, Joseph Martin provides a work of greatly expressive beauty.

35008914	SATB	$7.95
35008932	Preview Pack (Book/CD)	$16.95
35008916	Listening CD	$15.98
35008917	Orchestration	$350.00
35008919	10-Pack Listening CDs	$65.00
35008931	StudioTrax CD	$80.00

COVENANT OF GRACE
A Cantata for Holy Week or Easter
Joseph M. Martin

Incorporating new anthems as well as familiar hymns, the cantata celebrates God's faithfulness and his everlasting promises; appropriate for either Holy Week or post-Easter presentations. Approximate performance time: 45 minutes.

35004838	SATB	$8.95
35004842	Listening CD	$15.98
35004841	Preview Pack (Book/CD)	$16.99
35004848	CD 10-Pack	$65.00
35004847	RehearsalTrax CD	$64.95
35004839	StudioTrax CD	$80.00
35004840	Orchestration	$350.00
35004845	iPrint Orchestration (CD-ROM)	$250.00
35004846	Digital Resource Kit	$59.95

THE WEEPING TREE
A Service for Holy Week
Joseph M. Martin

The Weeping Tree is a poignant portrait of the cross that uses beloved hymns, newly composed music, thoughtful narration, and simple sacred symbols to create a touching testament of grace for choirs of every size. By offering the smaller orchestral accompaniment option along with the shorter performance time, *The Weeping Tree* is accessible to choirs that have not previously included cantatas in their Lenten and Holy Week services.

35022875	SATB	$7.95
35022877	Preview Pack (Book/CD)	$16.99
35022880	Chamber Orchestration	$250.00
35022882	iPrint Orchestration (CD-ROM)	$175.00
35022881	StudioTrax CD	$80.00
35022878	Listening CD	$15.98
35022879	CD 10-Pack	$65.00
35022876	RehearsalTrax CD	$64.95

FOOTPRINTS IN THE SAND
Joseph M. Martin

From the inspired pen of Joseph M. Martin comes a sacred work that traces the steps of the Savior from Galilee to Emmaus. Approximate performance time: 45 minutes.

35007055	SATB	$7.95
35007057	Preview Pack (Book/CD)	$16.99
35007056	Orchestration	$350.00
35007061	iPrint Orchestration (CD-ROM)	$250.00
35007065	StudioTrax CD	$80.00
35007058	Listening CD	$15.98
35007060	CD 10-Pack	$65.00
35007064	RehearsalTrax CD	$64.95

WE WERE THERE
Pepper Choplin

Versatile and adaptable to any performance time, a great resource! Maximum performance time: 50 minutes

35025251	SATB	$7.95
35025243	Preview Pack (Book/CD)	$16.95
35025245	Orchestration	$350.00
35025242	StudioTrax CD	$80.00
35025244	Listening CD	$15.98
35025241	CD 10-Pak	$65.00

ONCE UPON A TREE
Pepper Choplin

A work of great emotional depth told from the witnesses' perspective. Maximum performance time: 45 minutes.

35016181	SATB	$9.99
35016189	Preview Pack (Book/CD)	$19.99
35016186	Orchestration	$350.00
35016191	Accompaniment CD	$80.00
35016192	Listening CD	$15.98
35016185	CD 10-Pack	$65.00

SONG OF THE SHADOWS
A Service for Holy Week or Tenebrae
Joseph M. Martin

Song of the Shadows is an invitation to contemplate the love and sacrifice of Christ. Tracing in song the last days of the Savior, this work is a deeply moving worship experience. Approximate performance time: 35 minutes.

35021135	SATB	$7.99
35021157	Preview Pack (Book/CD)	$16.99
35021153	Orchestration	$350.00
35021156	Accompaniment CD	$80.00
35021158	Listening CD	$15.98
35021155	CD 10-Pack	$65.00